Bill Gates

In His Own Words

Bill Gates
In His Own Words

EDITED BY
Lisa Rogak

A B2 BOOK

AGATE

CHICAGO

First printing: January 2021

The Library of Congress has cataloged a previous edition of this book as follows:

Gates, Bill, 1955-
Impatient optimist: Bill Gates in his own words / edited by Lisa Rogak.
   p. cm.
Includes bibliographical references and index.
Summary: "A collection of direct quotes from Bill Gates on topics related to business, technology, Microsoft, philanthropy, and life"
--Provided by publisher.
ISBN 978-1-932841-71-8 (pbk.) -- ISBN 1-932841-71-7 (pbk.) -- ISBN 978-1-57284-704-0 (ebook) -- ISBN 1-57284-704-2 (ebook)
1. Gates, Bill, 1955--Quotations. 2. Businessmen--United States--Quotations. 3. Computer software industry--United States--Quotations, maxims, etc. 4. Business--Quotations, maxims, etc. I. Rogak, Lisa, 1962- II. Title.
HD9696.63.U62G37425 2012
081--dc23
                         2012022735

10 9 8 7 6 5 4 3 2 1   20 21 22 23 24 25

B2 Books is an imprint of Agate Publishing. Agate books are available in bulk at discount prices. For more information, go to agatepublishing.com.

This is how I see the world, and it should make one thing clear: I am an optimist. But I am an impatient optimist.

—BILL GATES

Contents

Introduction

L ove him or hate him, Bill Gates has been a venera-
ble worldwide business icon for more than three
decades, ever since the first mass-produced personal
computer debuted in 1981.

Alternately described as an ingenious visionary
and a tyrannical, sometimes less-than-scrupulous
businessman, he has been all but impossible to
ignore. But despite one's opinion of Gates, even his
most prominent naysayers have no choice but to
admit the obvious: he helped to spearhead one of the
greatest revolutions in modern history by turning the
inaccessible computer technology of the 1970s into an
invaluable and easy-to-use tool for the masses, while
also providing jobs and wealth to many along the way.

Gates has consistently been ranked as one of the
world's wealthiest men—as well as one of the most
controversial founders and CEOs in history—and
businesspeople of all stripes have taken their cues
from him, using his words and business strategies to
help create and grow their own companies. In 2008,
after Gates stopped running the day-to-day operations
of Microsoft to devote himself full-time to the Bill &
Melinda Gates Foundation, a kinder, gentler side began
to emerge—a contrast to his hard-nosed reputation. As
a result, people who are actively involved in their own
philanthropic efforts, whether in a professional or part-
time capacity, have begun to take a second look at the
man behind the foundation.

Despite the fact that he's no longer at the helm of one of the world's most powerful companies, Gates has steadfastly remained in the news. His friendship and philanthropic partnerships with U2's Bono and investing titan Warren Buffett attract the attention of both the media and public, which only helps to gain more attention for his charitable acts—whether he is testifying with former President Bill Clinton about increasing federal aid to earthquake-ravaged cities and villages in Haiti or making the rounds at the Sundance Film Festival to promote the topic of public education reform. And unlike Gates's days at Microsoft, where he was entrusted with protecting a bevy of corporate secrets, today his life is virtually an open book, featuring regular updates on Facebook and Twitter and blog posts at TheGatesNotes.com.

Bill Gates's second act is no less compelling than his first. Anyone interested in his personal life or looking for inspiration to drive their own business endeavors forward can find enlightenment through reading Gates's own words.

Part I

RUNNING A COMPANY

Early Days

THE EARLY DREAM was a machine that was easy to use, very reliable and very powerful. We even talked back in 1975 about how we could make a machine that all of your reading and note taking would be done on that machine.

—*What the Best CEOs Know*, 2005

WE DIDN'T EVEN obey a twenty-four-hour clock. We'd come in and program for a couple of days straight...four or five of us, when it was time to eat we'd all get in our cars, kind of race over to the restaurant and sit and talk about what we were doing. Sometimes I'd get excited talking about things, I'd forget to eat, but then you know, we'd just go back and program some more. It was us and our friends—those were fun days.

—*Triumph of the Nerds*, PBS, June 1996

LIFE FOR US was working and maybe going to a movie and then working some more. Sometimes customers would come in, and we were so tired we'd fall asleep in front of them. Or at an internal meeting I'd lie down on the floor, because I like to do that to brainstorm. And then I'd just fall asleep.

—CNNMoney/*Fortune*, October 2, 1995

WE HAD CONTESTS to see who could stay in the building like three or four days straight. Some of the more prudish people would say, "Go home and take a bath."

—*Masters of Enterprise*, 1999

There were a lot of missteps in the early days; because we got in early, we got to make more mistakes than other people.

—Smithsonian Institution Oral and Video
Histories, 2003

WE THOUGHT THE world would be like it is now in terms of the popularity and impact of the PC, but we didn't have the hubris to think that our company would be this size or have this kind of success. The paradox is that we thought, "OK, we can just have this thirty-person company that will be turning out the software for every PC."

—*Newsweek*, September 17, 2000

IF YOU HAD asked me at any point how big Microsoft could be, Paul [Allen] and I once thought we could write all the software in the world with one hundred people. If you had told us that someday we would have more than five thousand people writing software, we would have just shaken our heads.

—CNNMoney/*Fortune*, October 2, 1995

I WAS A huge beneficiary of this country's unique willingness to take a risk on a young person.

—CNBC Town Hall Event, Columbia University, November 12, 2009

Leadership

OUR BUSINESS STRATEGY from the beginning was quite different than all the computer companies that existed when we were started. We decided to focus just on doing the high-volume software, not to build hardware systems, not to do chips, just to do software...It was a strategy that required partners. I think the most successful partnership in the history of American business is the work we've done with Intel. When we started working with them, both companies were worth one-hundredth of what they're worth today. And so, working hand-in-hand in a nice, complementary way, you know, with a little bit of friction from time to time because we're both pretty strong-willed companies, we built two of the most successful enterprises of the era.

—Keynote speech, San Jose State University, January 27, 1998

I ALWAYS KNEW I would have close business associates ... that we would stick together and grow together no matter what happened. I didn't know that because of some analysis. I just decided early on that was part of who I was.

—*TIME*, January 13, 1997

IT'S A PHENOMENAL business partnership. I wouldn't enjoy my job like I do if it wasn't for how much fun Steve [Ballmer] and I have brainstorming things. And within the company, everybody has understood that we work very closely together and have a very common view of where we want to go.

—*Newsweek*, June 23, 1997

FEAR SHOULD GUIDE you, but it should be latent. I have some latent fear. I consider failure on a regular basis.

—*Playboy*, July 1994

WE DEFINITELY NEEDED to change. The last few years of trying to do both things [oversee product strategy and act as CEO] were pretty tough. [The transition] has worked out exactly the way I thought it would . . . I get more time on products than I've had for ages and ages. [And] there is a set of things that Steve [Ballmer] gets to worry about that I don't have to worry about.

—*The Telegraph*, February 1, 2004

PEOPLE ARE GOING to second-guess anything you do.

—*Newsweek*, August 30, 1999

[In high school I told the other programmers], "Look, if you want me to come back, you have to let me be in charge. But this is a dangerous thing, because if you put me in charge this time, I'm going to want to be in charge forever."

—Smithsonian Institution Oral and Video Histories, 2003

WE'RE VERY BIG on managers who are very much in touch with doing hands-on work, who appreciate the work that people underneath them are doing, and retain the skill sets to jump in and do some of it themselves. So they can understand what is the load like, what's hard, how's that going on, and pitch in when there is something that's particularly tough. We're big into managers that believe in a lot of communication. It's awful when you get a group that's kind of drifted, and the morale has gone down, and you wonder, why didn't you find out early, you know? You should always know that as soon as possible. And so managers really have to be in touch with all of their people.

—Keynote speech, San Jose State University, January 27, 1998

I LIKE QUESTION-AND-ANSWER sessions because they allow me to get a sense of what people are excited about and what they are upset about.

—*Industry Week*, November 20, 1995

EXTERNALLY, PEOPLE TEND to identify the company with one person. It's a natural thing so I've had mostly the minuses, but [also] the pluses of that.

—*Newsweek,* June 23, 1997

I WAS THE mover. I was the guy who said, "Let's call the real world and try to sell something to it."

—*Hard Drive,* 1992

Competition

PEOPLE UNDERESTIMATE HOW effective capitalism is at keeping even the most successful companies on edge.

—The Rich and How They Got That Way, 2001

CAPITALISM IS GREAT at having thousands of things going on in parallel. And a lot of them fail. Some are just mediocre. But the ones that are special can grow and, you know, stun everybody. And in all those fields I mentioned, there are going to be several companies that kind of take your breath away.

—CNBC Town Hall Event, Columbia University, November 12, 2009

IT'S EXCITING TO see what's going on in China. It's great for us. If we had a choice for all the people in China to be as rich as we are versus be as poor as they were back in 1979, we'd be way better off to say, you know, let's have them be consumers and inventors just like we are. They are a long ways away from that. But they are a large enough population that great things are happening there.

—CNBC Town Hall Event, Columbia University, November 12, 2009

THE CHINESE HAVE risk-taking, hard work down, education, and when you meet with Chinese politicians, they are all scientists and engineers. You can have numeric discussion with them—you are never discussing "give me a one-liner to embarrass [my political rivals] with." You are meeting with an intelligent bureaucracy.

—*The World Is Flat*, 2005

When you have the level of success that we've had, when you have a business that's as important as this, with this many competitors, you're going to have people saying some nasty things. And so you have to learn a little bit not to take it too personally.

—*20/20*, January 30, 1998

THE CHINESE ARE clearly inculcating the idea that science is exciting and important, and that's why they, as a whole—they're graduating four times as many engineers as we are, and that's just happened over the last twenty years.

—*Morning Edition*, **NPR, April 29, 2005**

IN CHINA WHEN you're one in a million, there are 1,300 people just like you.

—*TIME*, **January 13, 1997**

WHETHER IT'S GOOGLE or Apple or free software, we've got some fantastic competitors and it keeps us on our toes.

—*The Telegraph*, **February 11, 2010**

ALL GOOD CAPITALISTIC companies get up every morning and think, "How can we make a better product? What are they doing well? We're going to make it cheaper, better, simpler, faster." And great competitors spur companies on. And at every phase of our industry, it's been a different set of companies.

—CNN, October 5, 2008

I AM A devout fan of capitalism. It is the best system ever devised for making self-interest serve the wider interest. This system is responsible for many of the great advances that have improved the lives of billions—from airplanes to air-conditioning to computers.

—*WIRED*, November 12, 2013

WE TRY TO understand what other people are doing, even if their apparent mission is so distant that it is not obvious competition.

—*The New York Times* News Service/Syndicate, February 19, 1996

YOU BASICALLY HAVE to convince the other guys not to spend enough money to compete with us, to keep just making it harder and harder, move the terms up, we just keep raising the bar, and eventually maybe one of them will try to do stuff with us. But a lot of them will just say, "Forget it."

—Masters of Enterprise, 1999

YOU ALWAYS HAVE to be thinking about who is coming to get you.

—Showstopper!: The Breakneck Race to Create Windows NT and the Next Generation at Microsoft, 1994

"IF WE WEREN'T so ruthless, we'd be making more creative software? We'd rather kill a competitor than grow the market?" Those are clear lies. Who grew this market? We did. Who survived companies like IBM, ten times our size, taking us on?

—TIME, June 24, 2001

HOW HAVE THINGS gone since 1995? Have our sales increased? Have our profits increased? (Answer: yes, about tenfold.) Do we also wish we'd done everything that Google has done? Sure. But I'll take our track record since 1995 versus anyone.

—*Newsweek*, June 30, 2008

THERE CERTAINLY WERE a lot of other software companies. Within two or three years of our being started, there were dozens of companies. Some of them tried to do better BASIC. And we made darn sure they never came near to what we had done. There were competitors in other languages. They didn't take quite the same long-term approach that we did, doing multiple products, really being able to hire people and train them to come in and do great work, taking a worldwide approach, and thinking of how the various products could work together.

—Smithsonian Institution Oral and Video Histories, 2003

Technology is a boom-or-bust business, but it's mostly busts. I've always assumed that 10% of my technology investments will succeed—and succeed wildly. The other 90% I expect to fail.

—*The Wall Street Journal*, January 16, 2019

[GOOGLE HAS] SOME of the same problems we had. They are hiring a lot of smart people. They have gotten into the lead position in search, which is incredibly profitable to be number one in that. They may get a little competition as time goes forward. But they are a great example of what can happen, you know. Two young guys who got together, pursued an idea, and created a success that's absolutely gigantic.

—**CNBC Town Hall Event, Columbia University, November 12, 2000**

IT'S EASY FOR people to forget how pervasive IBM's influence over this industry was. When you talk to people who've come into the industry recently there's no way you can get that into their heads. That was the environment.

—*Triumph of the Nerds*, **PBS, June 1996**

THE RELATIONSHIP BETWEEN IBM and
Microsoft was always a culture clash.
IBMers were buttoned-up organization men.
Microsoftees were obsessive hackers. With the
development of OS/2, the strains really began to
show.

—Triumph of the Nerds, PBS, June 1996

[IT IS] A fast-moving industry and no one has a
guaranteed position...I like our position better
than others, but it's not in any sense guaranteed
in any way.

—InfoWorld, November 21, 1994

OUR SUCCESS HAS really been based on
partnerships from the very beginning.

—The Road Ahead, 1995

No ONE'S GOT a guaranteed position in the high technology business.

—*Triumph of the Nerds*, PBS, June 1996

WE WERE IN the right place at the right time. We got there first.

—*What the Best CEOs Know*, 2005

Company

Culture

YOU CAN'T JUST get a bunch of smart people together and know which path they should go off and pursue. Actually, it's amazing that that worked for the Manhattan Project.

—*MIT Technology Review*, September 1, 2010

I'VE ALWAYS BELIEVED in a paperless office.

—CNNMoney/*Fortune*, April 12, 1999

WE TELL PEOPLE that if no one laughs at at least one of their ideas, they're probably not being creative enough.

—*The New York Times* News Service/Syndicate, October 9, 1996

GENERALLY, CREATIVE PEOPLE like to work with each other. You have to make sure you're encouraging an atmosphere where the creative people feel comfortable, so you get positive momentum. A lot of people here have become very wealthy. We have to keep the place really fun. Otherwise, they have the freedom to go off and do other things.

—*Success Magazine*, October 1988

GREAT ORGANIZATIONS DEMAND a high level of commitment by the people involved. That's true in any endeavor. I've never criticized a person. I have criticized ideas. If I think something's a waste of time or inappropriate I don't wait to point it out. I say it right away. It's real time. So you might hear me say, "That's the dumbest idea I have ever heard" many times during a meeting.

—*Playboy*, July 1994

WHEN I GO to a meeting, I keep specific objectives in mind. There isn't much small talk, especially if I'm with colleagues I know well. We discuss accounts we lost or where overhead is too high, and then we're done. Bang! There are always more challenges than there are hours, so why be wasteful?

—*The New York Times* News Service/Syndicate,
February 19, 1996

TAKE OUR TWENTY best people away, and I will tell you that Microsoft would become an unimportant company.

—*Masters of Enterprise*, 1999

SMART PEOPLE ANYWHERE in the company should have the power to drive an initiative.

—*Business @ the Speed of Thought*, 1999

MICROSOFT'S AWARENESS THAT something very dramatic was going on around the Internet really came from an employee, so he became a change agent at Microsoft.

—*What the Best CEOs Know*, 2005

BELIEVE ME, WHEN somebody's in their entrepreneurial mode—being fanatical, inventing new things—the value they're adding to the world is phenomenal. If they invent new technologies, that is an amazing thing. And they don't even have to know how it's going to help people. But it will: in education, medical research, you name it.

—*MIT Technology Review*, September 1, 2010

OUR HIRING WAS always focused on people right out of school. We had a few key hires like Charles Simonyi who came in with experience. But most of our developers, we decided that we wanted them to come with clear minds, not polluted by some other approach, to learn the way that we liked to develop software, and to put the kind of energy into it that we thought was key.

—Smithsonian Institution Oral and Video Histories, 2003

WE LIKE PEOPLE who have got an enthusiasm for the product—technology—who really believe that it can do amazing things. We're very big on hiring smart people, so you'd better be comfortable working with other smart people, and kind of having the debate and questioning that goes along with that.

—Keynote speech, San Jose State University, January 27, 1998

We never waste a lot of time talking about what we're doing well. It just isn't our culture. Every meeting is about "Sure, we won in seven of the categories, but what about that eighth category?"

—*Newsweek*, December 1, 1996

WE [CAN] TAP into the energy and talent of five times as many people as we did before.

—*The World Is Flat*, 2005

IT'S ABSOLUTELY CRITICAL that we have an environment in which great minds from many countries can work together. We rely on skilled foreign workers for their math, science, and creative abilities as well as their cultural knowledge, which helps when localizing products for world markets.

—*The New York Times* News Service/Syndicate,
December 20, 1995

IF SOMEBODY IS very smart and contributing a lot, then it is fun. If they don't match that kind of level of energy, then it is really not the right place for them. It is an exciting thing. It is still a little bit different.

—Smithsonian Institution Oral and Video Histories,
2003

SMART PEOPLE OUGHT to be able to figure anything out if they get enough facts.

—*Showstopper!: The Breakneck Race to Create Windows NT and the Next Generation at Microsoft*, 1994

THE KEY FOR us, number one, has always been hiring very smart people. There is no way of getting around that, in terms of IQ, you've got to be very elitist in picking the people who deserve to write software. 95 percent of the people shouldn't write complex software. And using small teams helps a lot.

—Smithsonian Institution Oral and Video Histories, 2003

THE OUTSIDE PERCEPTION and inside perception of Microsoft are so different. The view of Microsoft inside Microsoft is always kind of an underdog thing.

— CNNMoney/*Fortune*, October 2, 1995

ONE OF THE great things about our culture is that we always operate knowing that projects we work on are key to the success and survival of the company. We've never had a culture where we say, "Boy, we're in great shape," because we know how dynamic the industry really is. We know we have to replace our products in a dramatic way. Or people will just keep using the current version of Windows or Office.

—*Newsweek*, April 16, 2000

[THERE IS] PLENTY of challenge, which is why it's good we're not a culture that looks back and has to waste a lot of time celebrating what we have done well.

—*Microsoft Rebooted*, 2004

We come into work every day knowing that we can destroy the company … and that we better keep our wits about us, make the long-term investments in research that are going to make a big difference and really drive things forward.

—Keynote speech, San Jose State
University, January 27, 1998

SIZE FUNDAMENTALLY WORKS against
excellence. Microsoft has long been an
aggressive supporter of small, focused work
groups. As the company has grown, we have
continually worked to have an organization
within an organization. Small teams can
communicate effectively and aren't encumbered
by a big structure slowing them down.

—IndustryWeek, **November 20, 1995**

WELL, HEY, WE can't do everything—we don't
expect to do everything. [But] we do a lot and we
have a longer time horizon than anyone else.

—PC Magazine, **June 23, 2008**

THE MONEY THAT companies spend on knowledge workers is a phenomenal amount. Whether those people do their jobs well is a huge part of whether the company is successful or not, so equipping them is not just a CIO thing. You've got to ask, "Are these clerk-type jobs?" Because if they are, they are likely to go away. Or "Are these thinking-type jobs?" In which case you should give the people pretty darn good tools and have the jobs be interesting enough that you can attract your share or better of the smart people to your company. That really is a business issue for the CEO.

—CNNMoney/*Fortune*, April 12, 1999

THERE'S NO ONE path at Microsoft. We have
a very flat organization. Sometimes ideas flow
down, sometimes they flow up, or horizontally.
Usually, someone will get an idea or identify a
problem and send e-mail to someone else. This
may kick off a SWAT team to deal with it. At
some point, the decision gets made face to face or
over e-mail. On strategic decisions, it may go to
a senior VP or to me. By and large, we empower
people to make decisions themselves.

—Information Outlook, **May 1, 1997**

WE WIN BECAUSE we hire the smartest people.
We improve our products based on feedback,
until they're the best. We have retreats each
year where we think about where the world is
heading.

—TIME, **January 13, 1997**

Business

Principles

WE'VE DONE A number of acquisitions in our history... A lot of the time, the reason we do the acquisition is, when we see a market developing very rapidly... we want to reduce the amount of time it takes us to get in there, get working with customers, get the feedback that's valuable.

—Keynote speech, San Jose State University, January 27, 1998

WE FOCUS ON what companies do well as opposed to what they do poorly. We don't dismiss a company as unimportant just because a lot of things about it may be less than perfect. The company may be doing something important; it may not even know that it is important.

—*The New York Times* News Service/Syndicate, February 19, 1996

THERE IS A tendency in companies to let good news travel fast. "Oh, we just won this account. Oh, things went so well." But, the thing about good news is, it's generally not actionable . . . Bad news, on the other hand, is actionable. "This customer is not very happy. This competitor is doing something very well. This project is behind" . . . The sooner you get the bad news, the better off you're going to be, in order to kind of absorb it, to change your product plan, to go back and talk to the people, really dig into it. So when somebody sends me mail saying, you know, "We won XYZ account for Exchange." I send mail back and say, "Does that mean we lost every other account, because you only sent me mail on one account? Tell me about the ones we lost, and why." And so that's really gotten into our culture.

—Keynote speech, San Jose State University, January 27, 1998

A BREAKTHROUGH IS something that changes the behavior of hundreds of millions of people where, if you took it away from them, they'd say, "You can't take that away from me." Breakthroughs are critical for us. All we get paid for are breakthroughs, because people who have our software today can keep using it forever and not pay us another dime.

—*Newsweek*, **November 24, 2003**

[A BUSINESS'S] CORPORATE memory is not very good unless somebody who is working on a project can sit down at their PC and in less than sixty seconds call up any memos or documents that might relate to a similar project that was done in the past. If it takes more time than that, people probably won't go and find it.

—**Speech**, *Enterprise Perspective*, **March 24, 1999**

ONE THING THAT never comes out is that the
software business is bigger selling to businesses
than it is to consumers. Microsoft is really in
touch with what are the practicalities, how do
you make workers more productive, what are the
pains in an IT department, what does corporate
site development involve. We have built up over
the decades the real ability to have great ongoing
dialogue with businesses about how they do their
software and what they do. We have a very strong
position.

—*PC Magazine*, June 23, 2008

YOUR MOST UNHAPPY customers are your
greatest source of learning.

—*Business @ the Speed of Thought*, 1999

I REALLY SHOULDN'T say this, but in some ways it leads, in an individual product category, to a natural monopoly where somebody properly documents, trains, promotes a particular package, and, through momentum, user loyalty, reputation, sales force, and prices, builds a very strong position with that product.

—Rosen Research Personal Computer Forum Proceedings, May 1981

THERE IS A certain irony that somebody says we have this enduring position that's unassailable, like some guy who owns the only copper mine in the world. The truth is very much the opposite. The company faces challenges, and we need to pull together as a team and do great work.

—*Newsweek*, April 16, 2000

Size works against excellence. Even if we are a big company, we cannot think like a big company or we are dead.

—on corporate strategy, *The Financial Times*, June 10, 1996

EVERY THREE YEARS are important in terms of redefining what we do. Any company that stays the same will be passed by very quickly and there are lots of fine examples of that...Because we now have a research group, and we are out there working with lots of universities and are able to continue to hire great people, I'm very optimistic about our future. But it is a future full of change and surprise.

—Smithsonian Institution Oral and Video Histories, 2003

THE BARRIER TO change is not too little caring; it is too much complexity.

—Commencement address, Harvard University, June 7, 2007

THERE IS THIS question on, say, a broad social issue: [do you] take the most controversial... position? When you have customers, shareholders, employees strongly on both sides of an issue that the company will not take a position on, this one, if it comes up again, we're going to go through a process and, you know, make sure that we're choosing to take a position or not for the right reasons. People can know what we stand for as a company in terms of anti-discrimination. They can also know that we won't necessarily take a position on every social issue that comes up.

—*Morning Edition,* NPR, April 28, 2005

WE WERE ALWAYS making the system somewhat more formalized. At some point you can't discuss every head in France and [have] the one guy at the top saying, "No, no, no. You want fifteen... you need eleven." You can't, you just can't, so eventually you have to delegate that.

—*Microsoft Rebooted,* 2004

THE ENTREPRENEURIAL MINDSET continues to thrive at Microsoft because one of our major goals is to reinvent ourselves—we have to make sure that we are the ones replacing our products instead of someone else.

—IndustryWeek, **November 20, 1995**

I'VE ALWAYS BEEN hardcore about looking at what we did wrong. We're not known for reflecting back on the things that went well. We can be pretty brutal about the parts that don't do well.

—Masters of Enterprise, **1999**

WHAT YOU HAVE here is, basically, the U.S. government saying our products are too capable.

—on the government's antitrust case against Microsoft, CNET, January 27, 1998

THE HARD-CORE TRUTH is that we've done
nothing wrong.

—on the government's antitrust case against Microsoft,
Playboy, July 1994

THERE'S NO DOUBT that we wouldn't have a DOJ
dispute here if some of our competitors hadn't
decided that battling it out in the marketplace
was that their product wasn't going to do well
enough on its own that way, that they were going
to try and use the government to cripple us. And
I use that word very carefully, because the idea
of trying to tell us to ship products with features
deleted, those are crippled products.

—on the government's antitrust case against Microsoft,
Keynote speech, San Jose State University, January 27,
1998

WHEN YOUR OWN government sues you, it's not a pleasant experience. I wasn't sitting there going, "Ha, ha, ha, I'll do what I want." I was thinking this is the worst thing that's ever happened to me.

— on the government's antitrust case against Microsoft, ZD Net, January 28, 1998

MANY PEOPLE WHO look at offshoring are looking to save costs. [But] that's not the key thing. It's the quality, the innovation, how quickly we get things done. If you look at the pipeline, it's going to be a tougher and tougher situation for us to hire. You want to have some diversity, particularly in research where you can draw on the talent pool that's there. There's no doubt that if we had easy hiring here in the U.S., we would be doing more in the U.S.

—*Morning Edition*, NPR, April 29, 2005

WHENEVER YOU DO a new piece of software
you decide whether it is data-driven or feature-
driven.... The key for Microsoft is that it is
okay for us to be early [with the launch of new
products]. We can afford to be early. What we do
not want to do is be late.

—*The Telegraph*, February 1, 2004

EVERY YEAR THAT we've existed, we've had the
excitement that this is a fast-changing business.
This wouldn't be a fun business if it wasn't
always risky.

—*Newsweek*, June 30, 2008

Don't make the same decision twice. Spend time and thought to make a solid decision the first time so that you don't revisit the issue unnecessarily…After all, why bother deciding an issue if it isn't really decided?

—*The New York Times* News Service/
Syndicate, October 8, 1997

THERE IS A huge responsibility to reach out, to be part of a broader dialogue to reach out to Washington D.C. and be part of the spam dialogue, to reach out to Brussels and share what we see coming down there. So in terms of the company being kinder and gentler . . . ever since we have been really successful, that's been very important. We get smarter about how to do it partly by making mistakes. We have the resources and the cleverness to look at those mistakes.

—*Microsoft Rebooted*, 2004

OUR DECISION PROCESS was very clear. There would be meetings I would be in, and we would make those decisions. And so there was no confusion, there was no politicking, there was no overly long memo trying to explain something or posturing. That's how we would make those decisions . . . You don't need a whole bunch of P&L owners or structure.

—*Microsoft Rebooted*, 2004

INSTEAD OF BUYING airplanes and playing around like some of our competitors, we've rolled almost everything back into the company.

—*Forbes*, March 23, 2015

MANY OF OUR mistakes related to markets we didn't get into as early as we should have. The constraint was always the number of people we could hire, while still managing everything, and ensuring that we could meet all of our delivery commitments. We were always on the edge.

—Forbes.com, December 1, 1997

PEOPLE DO PLAY computer games at work, but they also doodle with pencils. Do you take away their pencils? That's not the way a modern workforce is managed. You've got to trust people.

—*The New York Times* News Service/Syndicate, November 4, 1996

IF YOU TAKE quality as a given, you are always going to have some uncertainty in the date.

—on meeting deadlines, *InfoWorld*, November 21, 1994

I WAS ALWAYS thinking that the environment [where] we did product development should be a fun environment, a lot like a college campus. And this idea of using small teams means you want to give them all the tools, all the computers, an individual office, whatever it takes so that they feel like they can concentrate on their jobs and be very creative.

—Smithsonian Institution Oral and Video Histories, 2003

THE WHOLE PROCESS looked like a pain, and an ongoing pain once you're public. People get confused because the stock price doesn't reflect your financial performance. And to have a stock trader call up the chief executive and ask him questions is uneconomic—the ball bearings shouldn't be asking the driver about the grease.

—*Fortune*, July 21, 1986

MICROSOFT IS DESIGNED to write great software. We are not designed to be good at other things. We only know how to hire, how to manage, and how to globalize software products. The key was to never view ourselves as a service company. We had to be a product company. But it was an approach that would probably not apply to any other business.

—**Forbes.com, December 1, 1997**

WE'RE ALWAYS WORRIED about keeping our pace—staying ahead. We know all our products will be obsolete two or three years from now and that it's a very competitive industry where everybody wants to replace things we've done, and yet we're trying to grow and bring in new ideas.

—*InfoWorld*, **November 21, 1994**

We had ideas that the giants of the time missed. We're always thinking about what we have missed that could keep us on top.

—*USA Today*, August 24, 1995

FROTH IS MOSTLY good. It means that there are high levels of investment, and therefore there's a heightened pace of innovation and a corresponding fear of being left behind. That's almost a fad-type effect, but in this world there's a real phenomenon behind it that's pulling people into it, and that's good.

—CNNMoney/*Fortune*, **April 12, 1999**

WE ALWAYS THOUGHT the best thing to do was to try and combine IBM promoting the software with us doing the engineering. And so it was only when they broke off communication and decided to go their own way that we thought, "Okay, we're on our own," and that was definitely very, very scary.

—*Triumph of the Nerds*, **PBS, June 1996**

PEOPLE CAN'T COME and talk to me every day. And so they have to look to their Business Unit Manager, which is how we have it set up. Certainly, we are trying to preserve all of that culture, and get the advantages of being a large company with a broad product line, with stability, worldwide presence, great support, and yet have the advantages that a small software company has.

—**Smithsonian Institution Oral and Video Histories,**
2003

THE WAY OUR ladder works, you can keep getting promoted to new levels just by being better at creating the product. It's important to set examples. When something works out, you take the guys involved in that project and you make them heroes. You let everyone know that people should strive to be like them.

—*Success Magazine*, **October 1988**

I GOT TO the point where I couldn't look at all of
the code, which I had done in the early years. At
one hundred people, I knew everybody. I even
knew their license plates when they came and
went. I knew really what everyone was up to.
By the time it got to one thousand, that was no
longer the case. I was hiring the managers and
knew all of the managers, but there was a level of
indirection. And, certainly, as you go up over ten
thousand then there . . . are some managers you
don't know.

—**Smithsonian Institution Oral and Video Histories,**
2003

A LITTLE BLINDNESS is necessary when you
undertake a risk. You have to have a little suspen-
sion of disbelief where you say, "Hey, we're going
to do this unproven product. Let's do our best."

—*The Costco Connection*, **November 1997**

WE DIDN'T NEED a lot of formal process because, believe me, it's better to have three guys who really know what's going on than to have all of the processes that allow twelve to all sort of think they are part of that decision process.

—Microsoft Rebooted, 2004

SUCCESS IS A lousy teacher. It seduces smart people into thinking they can't lose.

—The Road Ahead, 1995

SMARTNESS IS AN ability to absorb new facts. To walk into a situation, have something explained to you, and immediately say, "Well, what about this?" To ask an insightful question. To absorb it in real time. A capacity to remember. To relate to domains that may not seem connected at first.

—The Rich and How They Got That Way, 2001

Part II

TECHNOLOGY

Machines

and

Software

IF A KID is addicted to a personal computer, I think that's far better than watching TV, because at least his mind is making choices.

—Programmers at Work: Interviews With 19 Programmers Who Shaped the Computer Industry, **1986**

ABOUT THREE MILLION computers get sold every year in China, but people don't pay for the software. Someday they will, though. As long as they are going to steal it, we want them to steal ours. They'll get sort of addicted, and then we'll somehow figure out how to collect sometime in the next decade.

—CNET News, July 2, 1998

COMPUTERS ARE GREAT because when you're working with them you get immediate results that let you know if your program works. It's feedback you don't get from many other things.

—The Road Ahead, **1995**

MEASURING TIME IS always tricky when you're someone who is on e-mail night and day.

—*Newsweek*, June 30, 2008

I READ A lot of obscure books and it is nice to open a book. But the electronic devices are good as well. Digital reading will completely take over. It's lightweight, and it's fantastic for sharing. Over time it will take over.

—*MailOnline*, June 12, 2011

IN EVERY PRODUCT we ship, the team knows of features that I asked them to put in that they didn't get in. So you never ship a perfect software product. Thank goodness you don't, because then what would you do?

—*Newsweek*, June 21, 2008

If you look inside my brain, it's filled with software and, you know, the magic of software and the belief in software and that's not going to change.

—*D5 Conference: All Things Digital*, May 30, 2007

IT'S EASIER FOR our software to compete with
Linux when there's piracy than when there's not.

—CNNMoney/*Fortune*, July 17, 2007

TO CREATE A new standard, it takes something
that's not just a little bit different; it takes
something that's really new, and really captures
people's imagination. And the Macintosh—of
all the machines I've seen—is the only one that
meets that standard.

—**Speech, 1984**

I'M VERY OPTIMISTIC about software. I can't imagine why software is not the most over-crowded field in the world. What could be more interesting than working on these tough problems and being able to have this kind of impact to build magic new devices? And, in fact, what I and my generation got to do these last thirty years really pales in comparison to what you'll be able to do in the next thirty years ahead.

—Speech, University of Washington, April 25, 2008

SOMETIMES I ENVY people who still get to program. After I stopped programming for Microsoft, I used to say half-jokingly in meetings: "Maybe I'll come in this weekend and write it myself." I don't say that anymore but I think about it.

—*The New York Times* News Service/Syndicate, March 14, 1995

The finest pieces of software are those where one individual has a complete sense of exactly how the program works. To have that, you have to really love the program and concentrate on keeping it simple, to an incredible degree.

—*Programmers at Work: Interviews With 19 Programmers Who Shaped the Computer Industry*, 1986

THE MAC WAS a very, very important milestone. Not only because it established Apple as a key player in helping to find new ideas in the personal computer, but also because it ushered in graphical interface. [Back then], people didn't believe in graphical interface. And Apple bet their company on it, and that is why we got so involved in building applications for the Macintosh early on. We thought they were right. And we really bet our success on it as well. And today, all of the machines work that way because it is so much more natural. But this was pushing the limit.

—**Smithsonian Institution Oral and Video Histories,**
2003

WHENEVER ANYBODY ELSE in the software industry wanted to know where we thought things were going, they'd come and talk to us. Because our vision, we shared; we didn't view that as some competitive edge. We just wanted to talk about it and get other people to share the same ideas so that they would help make it all come true.

—Smithsonian Institution Oral and Video Histories, 2003

THERE ARE ONE hundred universities making contributions to robotics. And each one is saying that the other is doing it all wrong.

—*The World Is Flat*, 2005

AMERICA HAS A lot to be proud of with this
industry. [Silicon Valley] has benefited
immensely. The jobs have been created here, the
wealth has been created here. You know, this is a
story that everyone should feel good about [and
that] the industry should feel good about.

—Keynote speech, San Jose State University, January
27, 1998

The Internet and Beyond

THE BEAUTY OF the Internet is its openness.
It cannot be controlled or dominated or cut off
because it is simply a constantly changing series
of linkages.

—CNNMoney/*Fortune*, March 3, 1998

PEOPLE GET CONFUSED. There is storage in
the cloud, which is clear that your file should
be up there and geo-distributed and backed
up, and there is computation in the cloud. The
one that you have to be careful of is what about
computation, because computation is not free.
But we are actually taking some pilot customers
and moving huge parts of their data centers into
our cloud where we manage it for them. Over the
next couple of years, a portion of the data centers
will start to move. Some people say data centers
will move to the cloud very quickly, but I tend to
think it will vary a lot.

—*PC Magazine*, June 23, 2008

I THINK SHORT of the transporter, most things you see in science fiction are, in the next decade, the kinds of things you'll see. The virtual presence, the virtual worlds that both represent what's going on in the real world and represent whatever people are interested in. This movement in space as a way of interacting with the machine. I think the deep investments that have been made at the research level will pay off with these things in the next 10 years.

—*D5 Conference: All Things Digital*, May 30, 2007

HEY, IF BEING a geek means you're willing to take a 400-page book on vaccines and where they work and where they don't, and you go off and study that and you use that to challenge people to learn more, then absolutely. I'm a geek. I plead guilty. Gladly.

—*MailOnline*, June 12, 2011

IF BEING A nerd means you're somebody who can enjoy exploring a computer for hours and hours late into the night, then the description fits me, and I don't think there's anything pejorative about it. But here's the real test: I've never used a pocket protector, so I can't really be a nerd, can I?

—*The New York Times* News Service/Syndicate, August 5, 1996

SOMETIMES WE DO get taken by surprise. For example, when the Internet came along, we had it as a fifth or sixth priority...But there came a point when we realized it was happening faster and was a much deeper phenomenon than had been recognized in our strategy.

—*Fortune Magazine*, July 20, 1998

IT'S EASY TO get spoiled by things that alienate you from what's important. I wouldn't want to get used to being waited on or driven around. Living in a way that is unique would be strange.

—*Playboy*, July 1994

Thank God for the internet. It helps you keep track of all the amazing things going on.

— The TED Interview: Bill Gates looks to the future,
May 2019

IT JUST SEEMS bizarre to me, the idea of a
60-year-old man trying to make hard calls about
where we invest in [research and development]
and how the pieces fit together.

—*The Telegraph*, February 1, 2004

WHEN I WAS young, I didn't know any old
people. When we did the microprocessor
revolution, there was nobody old, nobody. It's
weird how old this industry has become.

—*WIRED*, May 2010

JUST AS MOVIES entertain and move audiences,
the creation and acceptance of technology has its
own set of plot twists—often with uncertain or
surprise endings.

—*The Hollywood Reporter*, September 5, 2002

WITH TECHNOLOGY WE'VE always got that
people tend to overestimate what can change
in a year or two, and they underestimate the
cumulative effect of change that can take place in
a ten- or fifteen-year period.

—Speech, University of Washington, April 25, 2008

THERE'S NOT A single line of code here today
that will have value in, say, four- or five-years'
time. Today's operating systems will be obsolete
in five years.

—*Masters of Enterprise*, 1999

THE IDEA THAT us nerdy guys who work in fast
software, that we're supposed to have intuited
the social effects of all our things—you should
not expect that prescience.

— The TED Interview: Bill Gates looks to the future,
May 2019

THIS PERIOD IN the late '90s when people thought startups could do everything, people didn't care about research and the long-term effort required to do speech recognition, visual recognition. It got a little frustrating. All this capital was being thrown at those people, and they weren't really doing multi-product, long-term things, they were just kind of doing this one thing, but that was messing up the way that our work was looked at.

—*Newsweek,* June 21, 2008

THE IDEA THAT, in some respects, [technology] could be used in a way . . . that would come back into the realm of how people think about facts, or how they politically wall themselves off and lose understanding of other people—that was not anticipated.

— The TED Interview: Bill Gates looks to the future, May 2019

The increased productivity that will come from AI will create dilemmas about what should people do with that extra time, and you've got to consider that a good thing.

—CNN Business, June 25, 2019

TECHNOLOGY IS ONLY lightly connected to the classroom experience today. The view is that it could be used in a new way … You put these short lectures online for free and then you're actually going to that lecture part outside the classroom. And so you use the classroom time for problem solving if there is something you are confused about, or sophisticated ways of looking at the concept.

—*Black Enterprise*, October 2011

TECHNOLOGY IS JUST a tool. In terms of getting the kids working together and motivating them, the teacher is the most important.

—*Independent*, October 12, 1997

I'VE BEEN KNOWN to be too optimistic about some of these IT things in the past.

—*MIT Technology Review*, February 27, 2019

WE ARE NEARING the point where computers and robots will be able to see, move, and interact naturally, unlocking many new applications and empowering people even more.

—*TIME*, April 5, 2015

TECHNOLOGY IS STILL out of reach for many people, because it is complex or expensive, or they simply do not have access.

—*The Verge*, April 3, 2015

I MISS THE elegance of . . . writing super tight code. Almost nobody does that now because memory is so big that you people can be a bit more sloppy than you could be back then.

—*WIRED*, August 31, 2018

AND SO, YES, the world will need to have regulations about privacy and surveillance, and the companies involved should be part of that dialogue. But, no, they alone don't know all the answers, nor would you necessarily want them to be making the final decisions on that.

— **The TED Interview: Bill Gates looks to the future, May 2019**

TECHNOLOGY'S BECOME SO central that government has to think, ok, what does that mean about elections, what does it mean about bullying. . . ? So, yes, the government needs to get involved.

—**CNN Business, June 25, 2019**

WE NEED TO shape [technology] so that the benefits outweigh the negatives.

—**CNN Business, June 25, 2019**

It's pretty phenomenal that what was viewed as kind of a silly dream is now so commonplace.

— The TED Interview: Bill Gates looks to the future,
May 2019

Part III

EYE ON THE FUTURE

Philosophy

IT'S A GREAT irony that Brown v. Board of Education is viewed as a milestone in civil rights, and yet the difference in the quality of what the average Black student was getting in 1954 versus what the average student is getting today is not that great.... Some of the more outrageous [segregation laws were] easier to ... solve than this school thing.

—Ebony, October 2011

WHY ISN'T THERE outrage, absolute outrage over [disparity in the education system]? Why aren't there protests every day, I don't understand. Why wouldn't this activate people the way that it did during the Civil Rights Movement?

—Ebony, October 2011

[AMERICA'S] UNIVERSITY SYSTEM is the best. We fund our universities to do a lot of research and that is an amazing thing. We reward risk taking ... It is a chaotic system, but it is a great engine of innovation in the world, and with federal tax money [and] philanthropy on top of that, [it will continue to flourish].

—*The World Is Flat*, 2005

IT'S AN ABSOLUTE lie that has killed thousands of kids. Because the mothers who heard that lie, many of them didn't have their kids take either pertussis or measles vaccine, and their children are dead today. And so the people who go and engage in those anti-vaccine efforts, they kill children. It's a very sad thing, because these vaccines are important.

—on anti-vaccine proponents, CNN, February 4, 2011

Arming myself with knowledge and sitting down with people who live the topic and brainstorming with them, that's what helps me back the right people and make sure I know what's going on.

—CNBC Town Hall Event, Columbia University,
November 12, 2009

BUT CAN WE, by increasing efficiency, deal with our climate problem? The answer is basically no. The climate problem requires more than a 90 percent reduction in CO_2 emitted, and no amount of efficiency improvement is going to address that. As we're improving our efficiency, poor people are increasing their energy intensity. You're never going to get the amount of CO_2 emitted to go down unless you deal with the one magic metric, which is CO_2 per kilowatt-hour.

—*WIRED*, July 2011

IT'S AMAZING HOW strong a message is hidden in words like "diversity" or the broad term "corporate social responsibility." A company needs to have core values of who they are and what they do [which] makes employees feel they have a purpose and guides their action.

—*Creative Capitalism*, 2008

I'LL BE THE first to admit that it's very easy to make statements about this that sound good... There's a lot of room for fluffery in this space, and so you've got to bring in expertise and that will probably take a while to develop.

—*Creative Capitalism*, 2008

IF YOU BELIEVE that every life has equal value, it's revolting to learn that some lives are seen as worth saving and others are not. We said to ourselves, "This can't be true. But if it is true, it deserves to be the priority of our giving."

—Commencement address, Harvard University, June 7, 2007

THE CASE STUDIES of this crisis will be taught for decades to come. At least we'll get that benefit out of the pain we went through. Leverage is a very dangerous thing. Warren [Buffett] has talked about derivatives as weapons of mass destruction. That wasn't much heeded... And the mass destruction followed as predicted.

—CNBC Town Hall Event, Columbia University,
November 12, 2009

A QUARTER OF our teachers are very good. If you could make all the teachers as good as the top quarter, the U.S. would soar to the top of that comparison. So can you find the way to capture what the really good teachers are doing? It's amazing to me that more has not been invested in looking at how does that good teacher calm that classroom? How does that good teacher keep the attention of all those kids? We need to measure what they do, and then have incentives for the other teachers to learn those things.

—*Newsweek*, December 20, 2010

IF I HADN'T had great teachers during those years I wouldn't have learned how cool science and math are. In fact, I had a bad biology teacher and it's only as an adult that I've realized, hey, biology might be the most interesting science of all. But I stayed away from it.

—*Black Enterprise*, October 2011

SCHOOLS CAN HAVE an extended day [so that] if a student is having trouble with math work, there would be a set of videos he or she could watch and exercises to try out that are set up and personalized. And the number of adults who need to be around is quite small because a lot of the instructional pace is being driven by technology.

—*Ebony*, October 2011

WE HAVE TWO big theories about how we might…change things. One is to help improve the quality of teaching [which] means really studying why some teachers are so much better than others. There is some magic stuff being done by the best teachers. And yet there is not really an effort to transfer those skills to other teachers. One of the ways to change that is through…feedback. You get peers to come in and see what you're doing. If there is a digital camera in the classroom you can even review yourself.

—*Black Enterprise*, October 2011

WE CAN SAY that we want energy that costs, say, a quarter of what coal electricity does and emits zero CO_2. But there are many paths to get there, each of which a realist would look at and say, "Wow, there [are] a lot of difficult things along that path." It is disappointing that some people have painted this problem as easy to solve. It's not easy, and it's bad for society if we think it is, because then funding for [research and development] doesn't happen.

—*MIT Technology Review*, September 1, 2010

IF YOU'RE GOING for cuteness, the stuff in the home is the place to go. It's really kind of cool to have solar panels on your roof. But if you're really interested in the energy problem, it's [massive solar plants] in the desert.

—*WIRED*, July 2011

WHEN DISEASES AFFECT both rich and poor countries, trickle-down will eventually work for the poorest, because the high cost of development is recovered in the rich world, and then as they go off patent, they're sold for marginal cost to the poor and everybody benefits.

—*Creative Capitalism*, 2008

DESPITE OFTEN-HEARD CLAIMS to the contrary, ethanol has nothing to do with reducing CO_2; it's just a form of farm subsidy. If you're using first-class land for biofuels, then you're competing with the growing of food. And so you're actually spiking food prices by moving energy production into agriculture. For rich people, this is OK. For poor people, this is a real problem, because their food budget is an extremely high percentage of their income.

—*WIRED*, July 2011

WE NEED TOOLS that will allow women to protect themselves. This is true whether the woman is a faithful married mother of small children, or a sex worker trying to scrape out a living in a slum. No matter where she lives, who she is, or what she does—a woman should never need her partner's permission to save her own life.

—Keynote speech, 16th International AIDS Conference,
August 13, 2006

RICH COUNTRIES CAN afford to overpay for things. We can afford to overpay for medicine, we can overpay for energy, we can rig our food prices and overpay for cotton.

—*WIRED*, July 2011

THE NUCLEAR INDUSTRY has this amazing record, even equipment from generations one and two. But nuclear mishaps tend to come in these big events—Chernobyl, Three Mile Island, and now Fukushima—so it's more visible...The good news about nuclear is that there's hardly been any innovation in the past three decades, so the room to do things differently is quite dramatic...We basically say no human should ever be required to do anything, because if you judge by Chernobyl and Fukushima, the human element is not on your side.

—*WIRED*, July 2011

WE WILL REALLY have to screw things up for our absolute wealth not to increase.

—*The World Is Flat*, 2005

THE WORLD TODAY has 6.8 billion people. That's headed up to about nine billion. Now, if we do a really great job on new vaccines, health care, reproductive health services, we could lower that [forecast] by, perhaps, 10 or 15 percent, but there we see an increase of about 1.3 [per year].

—TED Talk, February 2010

IF YOU LOOK and say where is the greatest inequity, you have to take a global view of that. I mean, America stands for a lot of things. It stands for the innovation that a capitalistic society can drive. It stands for political freedom. But it also stands for ending inequity.

—CNN, October 5, 2008

THE WORLD IS getting better, but it's not getting better fast enough, and it's not getting better for everyone.

—*Creative Capitalism*, 2008

I THINK EVERY country in the world should make it easier for people with high skills to come in. I'm a big believer that as much as possible, and there are obviously political limitations, freedom of migration is a good thing.

—*Reuters*, March 21, 2007

THE GREAT ADVANCES in the world have often aggravated the inequities in the world. The least needy see the most improvement, and the most needy see the least—in particular, the billion people who live on less than a dollar a day.

—*Creative Capitalism*, 2008

HUMANITY'S GREATEST ADVANCES are not in its discoveries, but in how those discoveries are applied to reduce inequity. Whether through democracy, strong public education, quality health care, or broad economic opportunity, reducing inequity is the highest human achievement.

—Commencement address, Harvard University, June 7, 2007

IF YOU DON'T give it away, yes, I think some portion of it ought to be taxed, that there would be an estate tax. After all, the accretion of that fortune depended on the government's educational system, justice system. You know, it wasn't something where you just went off on your own and magically pulled some gold out of the ground.

—CNN, October 5, 2008

I WISH I wasn't [wealthy]... There's nothing good that comes out of that. You do get more visibility as a result of it.

—*The Guardian*, May 5, 2006

Industries are only valuable to the degree they meet human needs. There's not some—at least in my psyche—this notion of, oh, we need new industries. We need children not to die, we need people to have an opportunity to get a good education.

—*The Financial Times*, November 1, 2013

RIDICULOUS SUMS OF money can be confusing.

—*Playboy*, July 1994

WHEN I TALK about innovation, it can be abstract for some people. But the direct link between the challenges [a farmer] faces when her crop is destroyed and the solutions that [plant scientist] Dr. Ndunguru is working on every day makes it very concrete . . . That is why I say that innovation has been and will continue to be the key to improving the world.

—Bill & Melinda Gates Foundation Annual Letter, 2012

THE THIRTY MINUTES you used to spend reading e-mail could be spent doing other things. I know some people would use that time to get more work done—but I hope most would use it for pursuits like connecting with a friend over coffee, helping your child with homework, or even volunteering in your community.

—*MIT Technology Review*, February 27, 2019

PEOPLE CAN ALWAYS say, "Well, my country is such a small part of it—why should I make the sacrifice? Because I don't know for sure that the other countries are going to do their part of it." We don't have a world government. Fortunately, we don't have that many world problems—most problems can be solved locally—but this one is a world problem. Carbon is not a local pollutant. It mixes in the global atmosphere in a matter of days. So it doesn't really matter whether it's a coal plant in China or a coal plant in the U.S.—the heating effect for the entire globe is the same.

—*The Atlantic*, **November 1, 2015**

CLIMATE CHANGE IS coming, so we need to actually innovate ahead of the negative effects.

—*The Atlantic*, **November 1, 2015**

HOW CAN YOU not be interested in energy?

— **Stanford Energy Energy Investments Dialogue, December 2, 2018**

THE CLIMATE PROBLEM has to be solved in the rich countries. China and the US and Europe have to solve CO_2 emission.

—*The Atlantic*, **November 1, 2015**

IN THE MOVIES, it's quite different. There's a group of handsome epidemiologists ready to go—they move in, they save the day, but that's just pure Hollywood. The failure to prepare could allow the next epidemic to be dramatically more devastating than Ebola.

—**TED Talk, March 1, 2015**

IF WE START now, we can be ready for the next epidemic.

—**TED Talk, March 1, 2015**

If somebody cures cancer, you're not going to worry what country that comes from.

—Channel 4 News, April 20, 2017

IN 2015, I urged world leaders in a TED talk to prepare for a pandemic the same way they prepare for war—by running simulations to find the cracks in the system. As we've seen this year, we have a long way to go. But I still believe that if we make the right decisions now, informed by science, data, and the experience of medical professionals, we can save lives and get the country back to work.

—*The Washington Post*, March 31, 2020

IF WE LEARN the lessons of COVID-19, we can approach climate change more informed about the consequences of inaction, and more prepared to save lives and prevent the worst possible outcome.

—Twitter, August 4, 2020

IF WE FROZE technology today, you will live in a four degree Celsius warmer world in the future, guaranteed.

—*MIT Technology Review*, February 27, 2019

IT ISN'T ENOUGH just to develop powerful new medicines. They have to make their way from the lab to the hospitals, clinics, and homes where people need them. That journey doesn't happen automatically. Buying medical supplies and getting them where they're needed may sound easy, even boring, but it isn't. Saving lives in developing countries often means getting medicines to remote villages and war zones.

—*The Wall Street Journal*, January 16, 2019

I'M FOR A tax system in which, if you have more money, you pay a higher percentage in taxes. And I think the rich should pay more than they currently do, and that includes Melinda and me.

—*GatesNotes*, December 30, 2019

I CERTAINLY LOVE the IT thing, but when we want to improve lives, you've got to deal with more basic things like child survival, child nutrition.

—*MIT Technology Review*, February 27, 2019

I HAVE BEEN struck again and again by how important measurement is to improving the human condition. You can achieve amazing progress if you set a clear goal and find a measure that will drive progress toward that goal.

—Bill & Melinda Gates Foundation Annual Letter, 2013

YOU INHERIT A world that has already proven that progress is possible—a world that has rebuilt after war, vanquished smallpox, fed a growing population, and enabled more than a billion people to climb out of extreme poverty. That progress didn't happen by accident or fate. It was the result of people just like you who made a commitment that whatever else they did with their lives and careers, they would contribute to this shared mission of propelling us all forward.

—*GatesNotes*, May 5, 2020

THAT HUMAN ABILITY to take a much worse situation and craft it into the institutions and economic growth and innovation that we've had between WWII and now . . . I hope that this (COVID-19 pandemic) looks like that.

—*Vox*, May 26, 2020

YOU CAN ALWAYS use your voice and your vote to advance change. You can insist on policies that create a healthier, better future for everyone, everywhere—whether they live down the street or on the other side of the planet.

—*GatesNotes*, May 5, 2020

I WANT TO encourage software developers, inventors, and scientists to consider how they can use their skills to fight inequity. It's deeply rewarding. You get the chance to learn from super capable people—health care workers, farmers, political leaders—and work with them on tools that will empower them.

—*CNBC*, June 19, 2019

As a member of our global community, your actions can have a global impact. Whatever your professional goals, wherever you live, whoever you are, there are ways, big and small, that you can participate in making the world better for everyone.

—*GatesNotes*, May 5, 2020

Philanthropy

THE MOTTO OF the foundation is that every life has equal value. There are more people dying of malaria than any specific cancer. When you die of malaria aged three it's different from being in your seventies, when you might die of a heart attack or you might die of cancer. And the world is putting massive amounts into cancer, so my wealth would have had a meaningless impact on that.

—*MailOnline*, June 12, 2011

GLOBAL HEALTH IS our lifelong commitment. Until we reduce the burden on the poor so that there is no real gap between us and them, that will always be our priority. I am not so foolish as to say that will happen. But that's our goal.

—*The New Yorker*, October 24, 2005

IT'S REALLY DRAWN me in. And I find the same magic elements that made me love my work at Microsoft.

—*BusinessWeek*, February 12, 2009

I GET TO learn new things. But bringing top people together, taking risks, feeling like something very dramatic can come out of it—that's something that the previous work and the work now have in common.

—*BusinessWeek*, February 12, 2009

THAT'S HOW WE think about our philanthropy, too. The goal isn't just incremental progress. It's to put the full force of our efforts and resources behind the big bets that, if successful, will save and improve lives.

—*GatesNotes*, February 10, 2020

[ONE] WAY THAT running a foundation is not like running a business is that you don't have customers who beat you up when you get things wrong or competitors who work to take those customers away from you. You don't have a stock price that goes up and down to tell you how you're doing. This lack of a natural feedback loop means that we as a foundation have to be even more careful in picking our goals and being honest with ourselves when we are not achieving them.

—Bill & Melinda Gates Foundation Annual Letter, 2009

WE DO FAMILY planning. We fund research on crops. Some people think that you shouldn't take science to help the poor people. This whole thing about which operating system somebody uses is a pretty silly thing versus issues involving starvation or death.

—*Newsweek,* June 30, 2008

In giving money, you have to be as careful as you are in making money. You want to make sure it goes to good causes. And so, if you just spend it in an unthinking way, it can be gone in a second.

—*20/20*, January 30, 1998

WE DO NOT measure ourselves at all by the amount given. We have taken on the top twenty killers, and for everything we do we look at the cost per life saved and real outcomes in terms of how things get improved. It's fun, and it is also an enormous responsibility ... That is true for being a parent. Many of the most important things in life are like that. Why else would you want to get up in the morning?

—*The New Yorker*, October 24, 2005

IT'S ALL THE greater crime that something like malaria never got more attention. We gave a small grant at first, like thirty million dollars, and everybody said, "Wow! That is the greatest increase in non-government spending in the history of malaria research!" And I thought, oh, you are kidding.

—*The New Yorker*, October 24, 2005

THE FACT THAT malaria was eliminated in the United States and we don't need a malaria vaccine is a tiny bit of a tragedy because you don't have all of these brilliant minds at work to solve this problem.

—Creative Capitalism, 2008

IT JUST BLOWS my mind how little money has been spent on malaria research. What has prevented the rich world from attempting this? Do we really not care because it doesn't affect us? Human suffering as a result of malaria is incomparable. By many measures, it's easily the worst thing on the planet. I refuse to sit there and say, O.K., next problem, this one doesn't bother me. It does bother me. And the only way for that to change is to stop malaria. So that is what we are going to have to do.

—The New Yorker, October 24, 2005

THIS LEADS TO the paradox that because the disease is only in the poor countries, there is not much investment. For example, there is more money put into baldness drugs than are put into malaria. Now baldness is a terrible thing and rich men are afflicted, so that is why that priority is set.

—**TED Talk, February 2009**

YOU KNOW, IN a lot of philanthropy, things don't go very well.

—*Reading with the Stars*, **2011**

YOU THINK IN philanthropy that your dollars will just be marginal, because the really juicy obvious things will all have been taken. So you look at this stuff and we are like, wow! When somebody is saying to you we can save many lives for hundreds of dollars each, the answer has to be no, no, no. That would already have been done. We go to events where people are raising money for various illnesses where lives are being treated as if they were worth many millions of dollars. And here we were learning that you can save even more lives for a few hundred each. We really did think it was too shocking to be true.

—*The New Yorker*, October 24, 2005

IN THE EARLY days of the company I was very proud that we had no lobbyists ever, no PACs. I had to spend more time in capitals of other countries than our capital. What a testament that was to America. You could build a company with great success without involvement in political activities of any kind.

—*Microsoft Rebooted*, 2004

How do you make [philanthropy] a fun, engaging part of your life, where it's not just a guilt-driven thing, but rather you feel like you're bringing some of your passion and understanding to it?

—The TED Interview: Bill Gates looks to the future,
May 2019

PROFITS ARE NOT always possible when business tries to serve the very poor. In such cases, there needs to be another market-based incentive—and that incentive is recognition. Recognition enhances a company's reputation and appeals to customers; above all, it attracts good people to the organization.

—*Creative Capitalism*, 2008

ALTOGETHER, OUR FOUNDATION has spent $53.8 billion over the last 20 years. On the whole, we're thrilled with what it's accomplished. But has every dollar we've spent had the effect we've hoped for? No. We've had our share of disappointments, setbacks, and surprises. We think it's important to be transparent about our failures as well as our successes—and it's important to share what we've learned.

—*GatesNotes*, February 10, 2020

THE PRIVATE MARKET does a great job of innovating in many areas, particularly for people who have money. The focus of Melinda's and my foundation is to encourage innovation in the areas where there is less profit opportunity but where the impact for those in need is very high. That is why we have devoted almost $2 billion to helping poor farm families, most of which are led by women, boost their productivity while preserving the land for future generations.

—Bill & Melinda Gates Foundation Annual Letter, 2012

IF WE WANT to accelerate progress, we need to actively pursue the same kind of breakthroughs achieved by Haber, Sabin, and Salk. It's a simple fact: Innovation makes the world better—and more innovation equals faster progress. That belief drives the work my wife, Melinda, and I are doing through our foundation.

—*WIRED*, November 12, 2013

GLOBAL HEALTH WILL always be a core focus of our foundation. This work will only become more important in the future, as climate change makes more people susceptible to disease.

—*GatesNotes*, **February 10, 2020**

A DYNASTIC SYSTEM where you can pass vast wealth along to your children is not good for anyone; the next generation doesn't end up with the same incentive to work hard and contribute to the economy. It's one of the many reasons that Melinda and I are giving almost all of our wealth back to society through our foundation, rather than passing all of it along to our children.

—*GatesNotes*, **December 30, 2019**

At the core of our foundation's work is the idea that every person deserves the chance to live a healthy and productive life.

—*GatesNotes*, February 10, 2020

MELINDA AND I believe that driving progress is wealth's highest purpose. Even before we were married, we decided that we would use the resources from Microsoft to make people's lives better. Our wealth comes with an obligation to give back to society, and in 2020, we're committed to continue living up to that obligation: through our taxes, through our foundation, and through our personal giving.

—*GatesNotes*, December 30, 2019

THE WORLD FACES a clear choice. If we invest relatively modest amounts, many more poor farmers will be able to feed their families. If we don't, one in seven people will continue living needlessly on the edge of starvation.

—Bill & Melinda Gates Foundation Annual Letter, 2012

I THINK THE best example of picking an important goal and using measurement to achieve it is the vaccination work UNICEF did under Jim Grant's leadership in the 1980s. Few people may have heard of Grant, but his impact on the world was as significant as any profit-driven leader like a Henry Ford or Thomas Watson.

—Bill & Melinda Gates Foundation Annual Letter, 2013

WHEN PEOPLE KNOW the kind of impact their generosity has, they are not only willing but eager to help.

—Bill & Melinda Gates Foundation Annual Letter, 2012

Part IV

PERSONAL LIFE AND VALUES

Collaborators and Other Industry Leaders

I'D GIVE A lot to have Steve [Jobs]'s taste.

—**D5 Conference: All Things Digital, May 30, 2007**

IN TERMS OF an inspirational leader, Steve Jobs is really the best I've ever met. I mean, he can make people work, you know, more than they should. He's got to be careful. It's such a strong power, he can overuse it. You know, I always say to him, he's a first-class magician, and I can recognize him, because I'm kind of a second-class magician. It doesn't mean I can do what he does, but I can kind of tell, "Wow, that's powerful stuff." As far as I'm concerned, what he did...was just unbelievable. He drove that team to do something that was a fantastic contribution.

—**Keynote speech, San Jose State University, January 27, 1998**

THE WORLD RARELY sees someone who has had the profound impact Steve [Jobs] has had, the effects of which will be felt for many generations to come. For those of us lucky enough to get to work with him, it's been an insanely great honor. I will miss Steve immensely.

—*All Things Digital*, October 5, 2011

[STEVE JOBS], OF all the leaders in the industry that I have worked with, showed more inspiration and he saved the company.

—CNBC Town Hall Event, Columbia University, November 12, 2009

YOU KNOW, PEOPLE like Steve Jobs and I were born at the right time. We were kind of stubborn and talented in some dimensions, so we built organizations that got to really make that revolution take place.

— The TED Interview: Bill Gates looks to the future, May 2019

[WARREN BUFFETT] HAS this very refreshing, simple way of looking at things.

—*The Guardian*, May 5, 2006

WARREN BUFFETT IS the closest thing I have to a role model because of the integrity and thoughtfulness and joy he brings to everything he does. I'm continuing to learn from my dad, I'm continuing to learn from Warren, and many times when I'm making decisions, I try and model how they'd approach a problem.

—The Charlie Rose Show, December 22, 2008

WARREN AND I love [listening] to questions and talking about our optimism.

—CNBC Town Hall Event, Columbia University, November 12, 2009

I THINK WARREN has had more effect on the way I think about my business and the way I think about running it than any business leader. He's got a way of thinking long-term, a way of analyzing the business fundamentals that the way he does it. He makes it all seem so simple. Well, of course, you know, he's analyzing in all these factors, and he's thinking way ahead of everybody else. But there's an immense value gotten out of that, as well as enjoy him as a friend. He's just an incredible person.

—Keynote speech, San Jose State University, January 27, 1998

HE LOVES TO teach. He does it meeting with students. He does it in his annual newsletter. He does it when he's talking to me on the phone. It's a real gift that I admire incredibly.

—on Warren Buffett, CNBC Town Hall Event, Columbia University, November 12, 2009

WHEN I FIRST talked to [Trump], it was actually kind of scary how much he knew about my daughter's appearance. Melinda didn't like that.

—**Address to Bill & Melinda Gates Foundation staff, May 2018**

[TRUMP] WANTED TO know if there was a difference between HIV and HPV, so I was able to explain that those are rarely confused with each other.

—**Address to Bill & Melinda Gates Foundation staff, May 2018**

PAUL [ALLEN] WAS a quiet thinker. The main thing about Paul was he is so curious about everything.

—**The TED Interview: Bill Gates looks to the future, May 2019**

[PAUL] WAS A great, curious person and
saw what was possible. He also saw that our
combination of talents was really necessary,
that I like to get out there and hire people and
push things in a way that our partnership would
be pretty magical. And so, there wouldn't be a
Microsoft without Paul.

—The TED Interview: Bill Gates looks to the future, May
2019

PAUL HAD READ a lot of science fiction and knew
a lot of things I didn't.

—*WIRED*, August 31, 2018

[PAUL AND I] kind of took over the computer room [at Lakeside School] and taught the other kids how to program. We were writing huge, complex programs in BASIC.

—*WIRED*, August 31, 2018

PAUL [ALLEN] WAS my friend from the early days. And we are very close friends today and I'm sure we always will be. He is very idea-oriented. He and I would brainstorm about things. So even though I was running the business, it was a partnership. His role was very, very critical to so many of the transitions that we made. [But] there was always some strain because I was pushing people to work hard, including Paul.

—Smithsonian Institution Oral and Video Histories, 2003

[PAUL AND I] were true partners. We'd talk for hours every day. [Today] we like to talk about how the fantasies we had as kids actually came true.

—*TIME*, January 13, 1997

ANDY GROVE IS an incredible CEO. He's big on picking objectives and driving the company towards that objective. He's big on clarity. He is an engineering manager, par excellence.

—Keynote speech, San Jose State University, January 27, 1998

I TEND TO be a little more realistic. [Bono is] always saying, "Yeah, we can do this!"

—*TIME*, December 26, 2005

IT'S NOT ABOUT making himself look good. [Bono] really reads this stuff; he cares about the complexity. Look, Bono is really, really having an impact. Things would be very different without him.

—*TIME*, December 26, 2005

[ONE NIGHT BONO] was on fire, talking about how we could get a percentage of each purchase from civic-minded companies to help change the world. He kept calling people, waking them up, and handing me the phone. His projections were a little enthusiastic at first—but his principle was right. If you give people a chance to associate themselves with a cause they care about, they will pay more, and that premium can make an impact.

—Speech, 2008 World Economic Forum, January 24, 2008

STEVE BALLMER SAID... that the responsibility of being CEO was more burdensome than he had expected. Well, I told him before he took the job that it was an inhuman job. It makes infinite demands on you, and I feel very lucky that I have Steve. I think he's stepping into the shoes exactly the way I hoped he would.

—*Newsweek*, **April 16, 2000**

I HAD TO change. Steve [Ballmer] is all about being on the team and being committed to the mutual goals. So I had to figure out, what are my behaviors that don't reinforce that? What is it about sarcasm in a meeting? Or just going, "This is completely screwed up?"

—*The Wall Street Journal*, **June 5, 2008**

STEVE WAS SMART enough and personal enough, that even though he didn't have a technical background, the programmers accepted him. That was very rare. We didn't really believe non-programmers should manage programmers. But the developers accepted him early on because he was smart, he would sit and listen to them, understand the things that they really liked to do.

—**Smithsonian Institution Oral and Video Histories, 2003**

STEVE WAS SUPERCRITICAL, full of ideas, influencing everything we did—even technical things like how we would organize, what people we would pick. But I was the decision maker.

—*Microsoft Rebooted*, **2004**

The benefit of sparking off somebody who's got that kind of brilliance is that it not only makes business more fun, but it really leads to a lot of success.

—CNNMoney/*Fortune*, July 20, 1998

STEVE [BALLMER] HAD accepted that he wasn't going to get the visibility, the glory, and the final decision on anything. And I was good at saying, Steve, do you want to say anything more [while making decisions]? But I had to make the final decision.

—*Working Together: Why Great Partnerships Succeed*,
2010

STEVE IS MY best friend...He was the opposite of me. I didn't go to classes much, wasn't involved in campus activities. Steve was involved in everything, knew everyone...He got me to join the Fox Club, a men's club where you put on tuxedos, smoke cigars, drink too much, stand up on chairs and tell stories, play pool. Very old school.

—*Forbes*, January 27, 1997

I HAVE STEVE look at my calendar. It's a conversation we have at least ten times a year: "I'm feeling overloaded again. I wonder if I'm spending my time the right way?" And so Steve will get my calendar and flip through it and say, "Did you really need to do this speech? Did you need to meet with these guys?"

—*Newsweek*, June 23, 1997

Family

OBVIOUSLY, OUR KIDS have benefitted from having a great education and an opportunity to travel, and they're very lucky in that sense. Making sure that the visibility or the way people treat them is not unnatural—there are some challenges that come with that.

—**CNN Business, June 25, 2019**

MELINDA IS THE one who deserves any—or certainly almost all—[of] the credit for the kids, so far, doing very well.

—**CNN Business, June 25, 2019**

MELINDA'S A TOTALLY equal partner in all the foundation work we're doing... To have somebody to brainstorm with makes it a lot more fun ... Things like writing letters together, giving speeches together, we had to learn how to bring out the best of both of us in doing those things. But, yeah, it was always clear we wanted to do it together.

—*WIRED*, **August 31, 2018**

MY PRIORITY IN life is my family. I always knew I'd get married and have children. You know, family life is all about emotion and sharing things and doing things with each other.

—*20/20*, **January 30, 1998**

THERE WAS ONE point in my life when my mother was trying to explain to me about what color shirt to wear with what ties... And I think people listen to their mother's advice when it relates to fashion. It's not an area in which I claim to know more than she does... I don't look down at the color I'm wearing during the day. So if it pleases other people that I know a little bit more about which shirt to pick with which tie, that's fine... I think I know a little bit about it now, but below average.

—*Playboy*, **July 1994**

MY DAD HAS set an example by what he does... whether it was at the university, speaking out on tough political issues, or going to war, or being a great lawyer... He's the one who really got the foundation going, encouraged me to give early, got us involved in some very key causes, and helped us build what is now a strong group of people that I get to work with full-time. So my dad is somebody I aspire to live up to what he's done.

—**The Charlie Rose Show, December 22, 2008**

[JENNIFER, HIS THREE-YEAR-OLD daughter] is a little redhead with brown eyes, the happiest person I've ever met. Everything she does is just so fascinating. Just getting up in the morning... "Dah-dee, can I get up now?" So I go in and pick her up. I like carrying her around a lot and she likes to be carried around. She's just the perfect size for it, so she rides on my head.

—*Newsweek*, **August 30, 1999**

THE MORE YOU force them by picking your choice, the more they will go away from it.

—on raising his children, Pomona College, March 20, 2011

BUT I DON'T think it would be beneficial to them to have huge amounts of wealth. I think that's very distortive in terms of how you think of what the impact you're going to have, how you measure yourself, how your friends think about you and how they do things with you. And it's also bad for society.

—CNN, October 5, 2008

IT WILL BE a minuscule portion of my wealth. It will mean they have to find their own way. They will be given an unbelievable education and that will all be paid for. And certainly anything related to health issues we will take care of. But in terms of their income, they will have to pick a job they like and go to work. They are normal kids now. They do chores, they get pocket money.

—*MailOnline*, June 12, 2011

When you choose to get married and have kids, if you're going to do it well, you are going to give up some of the fanaticism.

—*WIRED*, May 2010

THE 12-YEAR-OLD IS always worried about the nine-year-old listening to songs with bad words. So he's like, "No! Skip that one!" So I only know some Lady Gaga songs.

—*MailOnline*, June 12, 2011

THE NICE THING about being a parent is it gives you a long-term perspective. You start thinking about, "Okay, you know, when my kids are my age, what will the United States be like?" I also think about my kids showing interest in different things—you know, I won't push them, but I'd love to have them be in some part of the sciences where they can make a contribution that really improves the world.

—*Morning Edition*, NPR, April 29, 2005

IN MY PARENTS I saw a model where they were really always communicating, doing things together...They were really kind of a team. I wanted some of that magic myself.

—*Newsweek*, August 30, 1999

MARRIED LIFE IS a simpler life. Who I spend my time with is established in advance.

—*Playboy*, July 1994

I KNEW NOT to get married until later because I was so obsessed with [the personal computer]. That's my life's work.

—D5 Conference: All Things Digital, May 30, 2007

[MY EXPECTATIONS] HAVE been completely fulfilled. I have a much more balanced life.

—on married life, *Newsweek*, August 30, 1999

AMAZINGLY, [MELINDA] MADE me feel like getting married. Now that is unusual! It's against all my past rational thinking on the topic.

—*Playboy*, July 1994

[FINDING A WIFE] certainly took me a lot of time.

—CNNMoney/*Fortune*, May 17, 1993

MICROSOFT'S COMPETITORS HAVE been quoted as hoping married life … will distract me from my work. After two years of marriage, that hasn't happened, and I don't think it will anytime soon.

—*Working Woman*, January 1996

[MELINDA] AND I enjoy sharing ideas and talking about what we are learning. When one of us is being very optimistic, the other takes on the role of making sure we're thinking through all the tough issues.

—*Working Together: Why Great Partnerships Succeed*, 2010

MELINDA AND I get very hands-on and involved in these things, and once we pick something, we like to see it through.

—Reading with the Stars, 2011

THE SIMPLEST THING to say about Melinda is that I fell deeply in love with her and decided to get married and have a family together.

—20/20, **January 30, 1998**

Interests

I AM A little obsessed with fertilizer. I mean
I'm fascinated with its role, not with using it.
I go to meetings where it's a serious topic of
conversation. I read books about its benefits and
the problems with overusing it. It's the kind of
topic I have to remind myself not to talk about
too much at cocktail parties, since most people
don't find it as interesting as I do.

—*WIRED*, August 31, 2018

THE WHOLE IDEA of how you run elections, and
how you raise money for elections, how you make
sure the voting system's working well—it's an
area for constant diligence because it plays such
a central role in our democratic process.

—Channel 4 News, April 20, 2017

THE ONLY ZERO-SUM game there is, is war.

—*MIT Technology Review*, February 27, 2019

I FEEL VERY lucky that I love digging into things like malaria.

> — The TED Interview: Bill Gates looks to the future,
> May 2019

I LOVE PLAYING bridge, it's a game where the players are aging quite a bit . . . it hasn't caught on with young people.

> —CNN Business, June 25, 2019

TIME WITH KIDS. Time with scientists. Time when I'm reading and things are making sense. Going out and seeing the impact of the foundation's work. Meeting with scientists who think we can make breakthroughs to solve climate [change].

> —on his greatest pleasures, CNN Business, June 25,
> 2019

WHEN YOU SWING for the fences, you're putting every ounce of strength into hitting the ball as far as possible. You know that your bat might miss the ball entirely—but that if you succeed in making contact, the rewards can be huge.

—*GatesNotes*, February 10, 2020

I EAT AT McDonald's more than most people, but that's because I don't cook... In terms of fast food and deep understanding of the culture of fast food, I'm your man.

—*Playboy*, July 1994

IT IS NOT a favor to a child to give them gigantic sums of money. It will, if anything, be confusing in terms of what their personal contribution and what their profession is and what they're going to get done.

—**The TED Interview: Bill Gates looks to the future, May 2019**

[FLYING COACH] COSTS less money. You get there just as fast as flying first-class. And my body fits. If I was really wide or really tall, I might view the issue differently.

—*The New York Times* News Service/Syndicate, August 29, 1995

WHEN YOU VISIT [my house], you'll get an electronic pin encoded with your preferences. As you wander toward any room, your favorite pictures will appear along with the music you like or a TV show or movie you're watching. The system will learn from your choices, and it will remember the music or pictures from your previous visits so you can choose to have them again or have similar but new ones.

—*TIME*, January 13, 1997

The distance between top and bottom incomes in the United States is much greater than it was 50 years ago. A few people end up with a great deal—I've been disproportionately rewarded for the work I've done—while many others who work just as hard struggle to get by.

—*GatesNotes,* December 30, 2019

I DEVOTE MAYBE ten percent to business thinking. Business isn't that complicated. I wouldn't want to put it on my business card. [I'm a] scientist. Unless I've been fooling myself. When I read about great scientists like, say, Crick and Watson and how they discovered DNA, I get a lot of pleasure. Stories of business success don't interest me in the same way. Say you added two years to my life and let me go to business school. I don't think I would have done a better job at Microsoft.

—Playboy, July 1994

YOU KNOW, WHO knows how history will think of me? You know, the person who played bridge with Warren Buffett, maybe. Or maybe not at all.

—CNN, October 5, 2008

I DON'T THINK that IQ is as fungible as I used to. To succeed, you also have to know how to make choices and how to think more broadly.

—TIME, January 13, 1997

IN MY TWENTIES, I just worked. Now I go home for dinner.

—*WIRED*, May 2010

I DON'T HAVE an iPod. A phone is a nice portable device to have your music on. Maybe some other people will think so too in the future.

—*The Big Idea*, CNBC, May 8, 2006

I'VE DONE THE same thing for thirty-three years, in a sense... It will be an adjustment for me. If I didn't have the Foundation—which is so exciting, and the work is complex—if I didn't have that, it would be tough for me, because I'm not a sit-on-the-beach type.

—*The Seattle Post-Intelligencer*, June 23, 2008

I THINK YOUR psyche about money is set by the
time you're in your early twenties. At this point
I'm clearly not by some definition "middle class."
Hopefully my psyche hasn't been too warped
in terms of the way I'll set my kids' allowance
and the way I'll think about what they should be
exposed to. It will be a lot like what my parents
did.

—*Newsweek*, August 30, 1999

IN NO SENSE would I say, "Oh, I'm making a
sacrifice because it's something my mother
told me I ought to do." I am doing something my
mother told me I ought to do, but it's going to be
a lot of fun. And I feel good about the impact as
well.

—*Newsweek*, June 30, 2008

BECAUSE THERE AREN'T enough hours in the day, it's tempting to try to do two things at once. Right now I'm perfecting reading a newspaper and riding an exercise bike at the same time—a very practical form of multitasking.

—*The New York Times* News Service/Syndicate, September 25, 1997

WARREN [BUFFETT] IS still somewhat better than I am. He plays a lot more than I do...about 20 hours a week. I don't get anywhere near that. In three or four years I will be a lot better than I am today.

—on playing bridge, *The Telegraph*, February 1, 2004

SOME PEOPLE ASK me why I don't own a plane... Why? Because you can get used to that kind of stuff, and I think that's bad. It takes you away from normal experiences in a way that is probably debilitating. So I control that kind of thing intentionally. It's one of those discipline things. If my discipline ever broke down it would confuse me, too. So I try to prevent that.

—*Playboy*, July 1994

I DON'T HAVE any TVs with their over-the-air receivers connected in my house. But when I'm in a hotel room or other places that have a TV, then I turn it on and flip the channels just like everybody else. I was watching cartoons on Nickelodeon on Sunday, *Ren & Stimpy* and *Rugrats*. Cartoons have improved a lot since I was a kid. I'm not immune to the lures of television. I just try to stay away from it because I like to read.

—*Playboy*, July 1994

PEOPLE MUST HAVE time to think about things.

—*Advertising Age*, September 23, 1996

WHEN I GO on vacation, although I do long-term thinking about the company, I don't do email. Email is the key to me. For me in terms of a real break it is when you're not doing email. At Christmas and two other times a year, I will have a vacation where, unless there is some real problem, I stay off email. There also better be a beach and the kids and some other things.

—*Microsoft Rebooted*, 2004

EVERYBODY SHOULD WATCH chemistry lectures—they're far better than you think. Don Sadoway, MIT—best chemistry lessons everywhere. Unbelievable.

—*The Seattle Post-Intelligencer*, June 23, 2008

Reflections

I'VE BEEN EXTREMELY lucky in the country I was born in, the education I got to have, the business work I got to do, even my foundation work is amazing and interesting work.

—*MIT Technology Review*, February 27, 2019

I'M SUPER LUCKY to have had two of the best careers you can imagine. You know, to be involved in personal computing and the magic of software, and now, our philanthropy, which spends most of its resources on the health of the poorest in the world—what's called global health—and we've had a lot of success there.

—The TED Interview: Bill Gates looks to the future, May 2019

I WAS A kind of hyper-intense person in my twenties and very impatient. I don't think I've given up either of [those] things entirely. Hopefully it's more measured, in a way.

—*The Financial Times*, November 1, 2013

I'VE BEEN VERY lucky. I've had two jobs that
were absolutely fantastic. When I was young,
writing software, staying up all night, you know,
dreaming about the personal computer I wanted
and I thought would be great for everyone,
that was the perfect thing for me. And now I've
switched. I'm totally full-time on the foundation.
You know, I'm loving advocating for these causes.
I'm making sure that the money our foundation
spends is—is used in the best way possible...I
love doing this work.

—CNN, July 20, 2010

I CAME TO be the leader of the antisocial group
[at Harvard]. We clung to each other as a way of
validating our rejection of all those social people.

—Commencement address, Harvard University, June 7,
2007

[THE TRIP TO the Serengeti with Melinda] was the first long vacation I had ever taken. It was a two week vacation, which seemed quite extreme to me.

—*WIRED*, August 31, 2018

HARVARD WAS PERFECT because . . . all night long there's people to talk to and they're very smart and interesting people . . . I almost even met a few girls, they walked near me, but I didn't talk to them much.

—*Inside Bill's Brain*, Netflix, September 22, 2019

I KNEW BEING a pure mathematician was not my destiny.

—*Inside Bill's Brain*, Netflix, September 22, 2019

EVEN TODAY, WHAT interests me isn't making money per se. If I had to choose between my job and having great wealth, I'd choose the job. It's a much bigger thrill to lead a team of thousands of talented, bright people than it is to have a big bank account.

—*The New York Times* News Service/Syndicate, October 27, 1996

I REALLY HAD a lot of dreams when I was a kid, and I think a great deal of that grew out of the fact that I had a chance to read a lot.

—*PC Magazine*, June 23, 2008

I TRIED TO be normal the best I could.

—*Hard Drive*, 1992

[TODAY], I WOULD rather be a genius born in China than an average guy born in Poughkeepsie.

—*The World Is Flat*, 2005

IT CONCERNS ME to hear young people say they don't want to go to college because I didn't graduate. For one thing, I got a pretty good education even though I didn't stay long enough to get my degree. For another, the world is getting more competitive, specialized and complex each year, making a college education as critical today as a high school education was at one time.

—*The New York Times* News Service/Syndicate, May 13, 1996

I STILL FEEL this is superfun.

—on continuing to work after becoming a billionaire, *TIME*, January 13, 1997

I'VE NEVER DONE anything solo, except take tests.

—*Working Together: Why Great Partnerships Succeed*, 2010

I CAN DO anything I put my mind to.

—*Hard Drive*, 1992

WE REALIZED THAT things were starting to happen, and just because we'd had a vision for a long time of where this chip could go and what it could mean didn't mean the industry was going to wait for us while I stayed and finished my degree at Harvard.

—*Triumph of the Nerds*, PBS, June 1996

I NEVER TOOK a day off in my twenties. Not one. And I'm still fanatical, but now I'm a little less fanatical. I play tennis, I play bridge, I spend time with my family. I drive myself around town in a normal Mercedes. I've had a Lexus. The family has a Porsche, which is a nice car that we sometimes take out. We have a minivan and that's what we use when it's the five of us. My eldest daughter rides horses, so we go to a lot of three-day shows. The kids are a big part of my schedule.

—*MailOnline*, June 12, 2011

HARVARD WAS JUST a phenomenal experience for me. Academic life was fascinating. I used to sit in on lots of classes I hadn't even signed up for.

—Commencement address, Harvard University, June 7, 2007

THERE WERE VERY smart people to talk to. They fed you every day. [But] you didn't have to go to classes.

—*Microsoft Rebooted*, 2004

PEOPLE'S PERCEPTION OF the importance of my role is certainly greater than the reality.

—*Newsweek*, December 1, 1996

THE WORLD HAS had a tendency to focus a disproportionate amount of attention on me.

—*U.S. News & World Report*, June 16, 2006

LEGACY IS A stupid thing! I don't want a legacy. If people look and see that childhood deaths dropped from nine million a year to four million because of our investment, then wow!

—*MailOnline*, June 12, 2011

RADCLIFFE WAS A great place to live. There were more women up there, and most of the guys were math-science types. That combination offered me the best odds, if you know what I mean. That's where I learned the sad lesson that improving your odds doesn't guarantee success.

—Commencement address, Harvard University, June 7, 2007

IT IS UNUSUAL to have so much luck in one life, I think. But it's been a major factor in what I have been able to do.

—CNBC Town Hall Event, Columbia University, November 12, 2009

I wouldn't trade places with anyone, but the reason I like my job so much is that we have to constantly stay on top of those things.

—*Triumph of the Nerds*, PBS, June 1996

NOT MUCH.

—on what makes him mad, *The Big Idea*, CNBC, May 8, 2006

I'M NOT BIG on to-do lists.

—CNNMoney/*Fortune*, April 7, 2006

I BELIEVE IN intensity.

—*Hackers: Heroes of the Computer Revolution: 25th Anniversary Edition*, 2010

I DON'T HAVE any particular goal for how I'm perceived. In writing [*The Road Ahead*], I'm sharing my thoughts, you know, my optimism and sort of the way I think about the business challenges and some of the changes. I've never written down how I want people to think about me.

—*The Washington Post*, December 3, 1995

WHEN SOMEBODY'S SUCCESSFUL, people leap to simple explanations that might make sense. So you get these myths. People love to have any little story. Yes, I'm intense. I'm energetic. I like to understand what our market position is. But then it gets turned into this—the ultra-competitor. It's somewhat dehumanizing. I read that and say, I don't know that guy.

—*Newsweek*, August 30, 1999

I'VE BEEN WAITING more than thirty years to say this: "Dad, I always told you I'd come back and get my degree."

—Commencement address, Harvard University, June 7, 2007

I WANT TO thank Harvard for this timely honor. I'll be changing my job next year . . . and it will be nice to finally have a college degree on my resume.

—Commencement address, Harvard University, June 7, 2007

I don't waste much time ruing the past. I made my decision, and the way to do it best is, once you make it, you just don't waver at all.... Being hardcore and forward looking about what you do is a necessary element of doing it well.

—*Forbes*, February 28, 1994

IN TERMS OF doing things I take a fairly scientific approach to why things happen and how they happen. I don't know if there's a god or not, but I think religious principles are quite valid.

—Talking with David Frost: Bill Gates, **1995**

I WAS RAISED religiously. And my wife and I definitely believe in raising our kids religiously. I'm a big believer in religious values. As far as, you know, the deep questions about God, it's not something that I think I personally have the answers to.

—20/20, **January 30, 1998**

JUST IN TERMS of allocation of time resources, religion is not very efficient. There's a lot more I could be doing on a Sunday morning.

—TIME, **January 13, 1997**

I CERTAINLY WILL never be a politician … for every reason. I wouldn't be elected, I'm better at what I'm doing. Whether it's time spent on Microsoft or the foundation … I'm going to stick to what I know.

—*The Big Idea*, CNBC, May 8, 2006

THERE BECOME A few magic moments where you have to have confidence in yourself … When I dropped out of Harvard and said to my friends, "Come work for me," there was a certain kind of brass self-confidence in that. You have a few moments like that where trusting yourself and saying yes, this can come together—you have to seize on those because not many come along.

—CNBC Town Hall Event, Columbia University, November 12, 2009

THE HARD-CORE YEARS, the most fanatical years, are thirteen to sixteen. By the time I was seventeen, my software mind had been shaped.

—*Hackers: Heroes of the Computer Revolution*, 2010

BULLSHIT.

—on whether he's mellowed in recent years, *The Seattle Post-Intelligencer*, June 23, 2008

IF YOU SAY, "Gosh, I won't leave when there's an interesting competitor," then you'd have to die on the job.

—*Newsweek*, June 21, 2008

IT'S POSSIBLE, you can never know, that the universe exists only for me. If so, it's sure going well for me, I must admit.

—*TIME*, January 13, 1997

I'M AN OPTIMIST. I think this is a wonderful time to be alive. There have never been so many opportunities to do things that were impossible before.

—*The Road Ahead*, 1995

MILESTONES

1955

- William Henry Gates III is born in Seattle to William H. and Mary Maxwell Gates. (October 28)

1967

- Gates—nicknamed Trey because his father Bill Gates Sr. customarily used the suffix II after his name—begins attending Lakeside School, a private college preparatory school where many children from Seattle's wealthy and elite families were enrolled, including Paul Allen.

- Gates uses a computer for the first time.

1968

- At age thirteen, Gates writes his first computer program in BASIC on an old Teletype Model 33 terminal at school.

1970

- Gates starts a business with Paul Allen. Their main product is "Traf-o-Data," a program to help keep tabs on traffic patterns.

1972

- Gates works as a congressional page in the United States House of Representatives over the summer.

1973

- Gates graduates from Lakeside in June after scoring 1590 out of 1600 points on the SAT. He is accepted into the pre-law program at Harvard University.

- Gates becomes friends with Steve Ballmer, who lives in the same dorm.

1974

- Gates takes a summer job with electronics firm Honeywell, joining Paul Allen, who had dropped out of college to work there.

1975

- An article about the Altair 8800, manufactured by Micro Instrumentation and Telemetry Systems— MITS—appears in Popular Electronics, captivating Gates. He and Paul Allen write BASIC software for the computer, and the manufacturer—based in Albuquerque—hires the pair.

- Gates leaves Harvard in his junior year and moves to Albuquerque with Allen; they christen their partnership Micro-Soft.

1976

- Gates and Allen officially register Microsoft—without the hyphen—as a business organization. Computer hobbyists had acquired copies of BASIC, which they used and passed along to others, without paying Microsoft. Gates writes a scathing letter accusing the hobbyists of theft.

1977

- Microsoft severs ties with MITS. Gates writes and develops other computer languages including FOR-TRAN for various companies and contractors.

- Gates is arrested in Albuquerque for speeding.

1978

- Microsoft opens its first international office, in Japan.

- Company revenues hit $1 million.

1979

- Microsoft moves its offices to Bellevue, Washington. Twenty-five employees work full-time for the company, which generates $2.5 million in revenue that year.

1980

- Microsoft strikes a deal with IBM to provide the DOS operating system software for their line of personal computers, scheduled to be produced and sold the following year. Gates retains the rights to MS-DOS, allowing Microsoft to license the operating system to other PC manufacturers.

- Steve Ballmer joins Microsoft as personal assistant to Gates.

1981

- Microsoft officially becomes a corporation, naming Gates as chairman and CEO. Ballmer becomes executive vice president of sales and support. Gates receives fifty-three percent of Microsoft, Allen receives thirty-one percent, and Ballmer receives eight percent.

- The IBM Personal Computer debuts. (August)

- Microsoft has one hundred twenty-eight employees and an annual revenue of $16 million.

- Steve Jobs of Apple Computer asks Gates and Microsoft to develop software for their new computer named the Macintosh.

1983

- Instead of announcing a "Man of the Year," *TIME* names the personal computer as "Machine of the Year."

- Paul Allen is diagnosed with Hodgkin's disease and leaves Microsoft.

1984

- Apple Computer launches the Macintosh. (January)

1985

- The first incarnation of Windows launches, which many believe is similar to the Macintosh interface. (November 20)

- Annual revenue hits $140 million; 910 employees work at Microsoft.

1986

- Microsoft's first common stock is issued. With forty-five percent of the 24.7 million shares issued, Gates earns $234 million the first day of trading.

- BG moves Microsoft's 1,200 employees from Bellevue to new headquarters in Redmond, Washington.

- At thirty-one, Gates becomes the youngest billionaire in history.

1987

- *Forbes* names Gates a billionaire in its annual list of 400 Richest People.

- Gates meets Melinda French, a Microsoft product manager, at a Microsoft event in New York City.

1988

- Apple sues Microsoft, accusing Gates and the company of designing Windows to mimic the Macintosh design too closely.

1989

- Gates launches Corbis, a digital archive of art and photography.

- Microsoft introduces Microsoft Office, which incorporates several software programs, including Word and Excel.

1990

- Microsoft launches Windows 3.0. As a result of its overwhelming popularity—more than one hundred thousand copies sell in just two weeks—annual sales at Microsoft reach $1 billion for the year.

- Though Microsoft has been developing an operating system with IBM called OS/2, the company pulls out in order to concentrate on Windows.

- The Federal Trade Commission starts looking into anticompetitive practices between Microsoft and IBM.

1992

- Gates hits the top of the Forbes 400 list, becoming the richest person in the United States, with $6.3 billion in personal wealth.

1993

- Gates proposes marriage to Melinda French, who says yes.

- The FTC decides to pass on the antitrust issue, instead referring it to the Department of Justice.

1994

- Gates marries Melinda French in Lanai, Hawaii. (January 1)

- Gates buys Leonardo da Vinci's Codex Leicester for $30.8 million at auction.

- Gates launches the William H. Gates Foundation, officially marking the start of his philanthropic career.

- Mary Gates, Gates's mother, dies of breast cancer. (June)

1995

- Windows 95 launches; it incorporates the web browser Internet Explorer. (January 1)

- Gates's first book is published. *The Road Ahead* hits number one on the *New York Times* bestseller list and stays there for almost two months.

- His fortune pegged at $12.9 billion, Gates is named by *Forbes* as the richest man in the world.

- After not taking it seriously at first, Gates sends Microsoft executives a memo directing them to focus on developing software for the Internet.

1996

- A daughter, Jennifer Katharine, is born. (April 26)

- Warren Buffett replaces Gates as the world's richest man as declared by *Forbes*. Gates drops to second place.

- Internet Explorer 3.0 launches.

- Netscape, a company developing a browser, requests that the Justice Department look into Microsoft for bundling Internet Explorer with Windows.

1997

- After seven years of construction, Gates moves his family into a sixty-six thousand-square-foot house on Lake Washington in Medina. It's estimated that the house cost $97 million to build.

1998

- Microsoft launches Windows 98.

- Steve Ballmer becomes president of Microsoft.

- The U.S. Department of Justice and twenty state's attorneys file an antitrust suit against Microsoft, accusing the company of participating in anti-competitive practices.

1999

- A son, Rory John, is born. (May 23)

- Gates's second book, *Business @ the Speed of Thought*, is published in twenty-five languages.

2000

- Microsoft launches two separate versions of Windows: 2000 and Me, short for Millennium Edition.

- Gates passes his title of Microsoft CEO to Steve Ballmer; Gates officially becomes known as Chief Software Architect.

- The judge in the antitrust trial orders Microsoft to become two companies; one for Windows and one for all other software. Gates appeals the ruling.

- Gates and his wife launch the Bill & Melinda Gates Foundation, incorporating several other foundations, with an initial contribution of $16 billion from personal funds.

- Global annual revenues for Microsoft hit $229 billion; the number of employees is almost forty thousand.

2001

- The judge's decision in the antitrust trial is overturned. Microsoft and the Department of Justice reach an agreement that keeps the company intact.

- Windows XP is introduced.

- Microsoft launches the Xbox, a video game console.

2002

- A daughter, Phoebe Adele, is born.

2004

- Gates becomes a board member at Berkshire Hathaway, his friend Warren Buffett's investment business.

- The European Commission launches an antitrust investigation of Microsoft.

2005

- *TIME* names Bill and Melinda Gates and U2's Bono as its Persons of the Year because of their philanthropic work.

- Gates receives an honorary knighthood from Queen Elizabeth.

2006

- Warren Buffett gives the bulk of his wealth, $31 billion, to the Bill & Melinda Gates Foundation.

- Gates announces that he will step down from his full-time job at Microsoft in 2008.

- Gates receives the 2006 James C. Morgan Global Humanitarian Award.

2007

- Gates receives an honorary Doctor of Law degree from Harvard; he gives the commencement speech at the ceremony.

- Microsoft introduces Windows Vista and Office 2007.

2008

- The European Union fines Microsoft $1.4 billion, claiming the company has not followed through on an earlier EU ruling, ordering the company to give specific software code to its competitors.

- Gates spends his last day at Microsoft. He stays on as chairman. (June 27)

- The number of Microsoft employees hits ninety thousand.

2009

- Despite losing $18 billion in net worth, Gates usurps buddy Warren Buffett as *Forbes'* number-one billionaire in the world, retaining $40 billion in personal wealth.

- Gates quits using Facebook because too many people want to friend him.

2010

- Gates attends the Sundance Film Festival to help promote *Waiting for Superman*, a documentary that he helped to fund about America's failing education system.

- Gates rejoins Facebook and signs up for Twitter as well.

2011

- Gates loses the top spot on *Forbes*' list of the richest people in the world because he's given away so much money; he's still second on the list, with $53 billion; Buffett is third for the year. Gates is still the wealthiest American.

- Rumors swirl late in the year that Gates will return to Microsoft. No dice, he says; he likes his foundation work too much.

2013

- Gates supports a six-year, $5.5 billion effort to eradicate polio by 2018.

2015

- Gates gives a TED talk which predicts a global pandemic along the lines of COVID-19.

2016

- Bill and Melinda Gates receive the Presidential Medal of Freedom from President Obama.

2017

- The Bill & Melinda Gates Foundation commits $300 million to helping farmers in Africa and Asia cope with climate change.

- Gates announces he is investing $50 million in the Dementia Discovery Fund.

- Gates plays as Roger Federer's doubles partner at the "Match for Africa: Seattle" fundraiser. The event raised over $2 million for the Roger Federer Foundation. (They teamed up again in 2020 in Cape Town, playing against Rafael Nadal and Trevor Noah.)

2018

- As of this year, the Bill & Melinda Gates Foundation has a $46.8 billion endowment, making it one of the world's largest private charitable organizations.

2020

- Gates ranks number two on *Forbes'* list of billionaires, with a net worth of $98 billion.

- The Bill & Melinda Gates Foundation commits $250 million to slow the spread of COVID-19.